Q8.50x08.50_10 PING-SS_G 9781739648527
76.1974LVX003306B
76.1974LV000022B

This Book Belongs To:

The First Thanksgiving

of 1621

By Stephanie O'Connor & Matthew O'Connor

First Edition published in 2020
This hardback edition published in 2023 by Madra Rua Publishing
ISBN: 978-1-7396485-2-7

www.madraruapublishing.com

In 1620 the Pilgrims traveled from England to America on a ship called the *Mayflower*.

All through the first summer in America, and the early part of autumn, the Pilgrims were busy and happy. They had planted and cared for their first fields of corn.

They had found wild strawberries in the meadows, raspberries on the hillsides, and wild grapes in the woods.

In the forest just back of Plymouth village wild turkeys and deer were caught for food.

In the rivers, lakes and shallow
waters of the bay, there was plenty
of fish, clams and lobsters to eat.

The warm summer sunshine and rain had left autumn with a fine crop of corn. The Pilgrims also harvested onions, beans, cabbage and carrots.

"Let's gather the food from our first harvest and celebrate together," said Governor Bradford.

Elder Brewster agreed. They would take time to thank God for their blessings. In fact, the Pilgrims thought that one day was not enough to give thanks, so they planned to have a celebration for a whole week!

The Pilgrims invited their Native American friends who had been so kind to them.

The native people knew the land well and had fished, hunted, and harvested for thousands of generations. And the New England Native American tribes already had autumn harvest feasts of thanksgiving to the Creator. This was an opportunity to join together in thanks and praise.

The Great Native American Leader, Massasoit, came with ninety of his bravest warriors.

Men went out to hunt wild turkeys and Massasoit sent some of his best hunters into the woods to hunt deer, which they gave to their pilgrim friends for the celebrations.

They built fires to cook the food.

They all gathered together.

Long tables were built under the trees on which were piled big plates of roast turkey, deer meat, baked clams, broiled fish and pumpkin.

What a happy time everybody had during that week! As well as great meals, there was lots of fun. In the daytime, the young men ran races and played games, while every night there was singing and dancing.

Sadly, on the third day, it was time for Great Leader Massasoit and his warriors to leave. The Pilgrims had a service of prayer and praise.

Massasoit and his warriors said goodbye to their Pilgrim friends and began their journey home to Mount Hope Bay.

The first Thanksgiving of 1621 took place nearly four hundred years ago. Since that time, Thanksgiving has been kept as a tradition by the people of New England and across America as a time to pause, give thanks, and as a season of blessed memories.

At this time, when the autumn wind scatters the leaves, families come together for the last Thursday in November to celebrate the official Thanksgiving Day, a national holiday honoring the early settlers and Native Americans who once came together to have a historic harvest feast.

A table is set, and family members sit side by side. For many, the traditional Thanksgiving meal includes seasonal dishes such as roast turkey with stuffing, cranberry sauce, mashed potatoes and pumpkin pie. At Thanksgiving, people often take the time to be with family and friends and give thanks to their God, and for all the blessings in their lives.

Printed in the USA
CPSIA information can be obtained
at www.ICGtesting.com
LVRC090806251023
761974LV00022B/306